ILLUMINATED SOULS

Finding Allah's Essence in Creation

Zaytoona Nur

Copyright © *Zaytoona Nur,* 2025
All Rights Reserved

This book is subject to the condition that no part of this book is to be reproduced, transmitted in any form or means; electronic or mechanical, stored in a retrieval system, photocopied, recorded, scanned, or otherwise. Any of these actions require the proper written permission of the author.

Table of Contents

Chapter 1: The Invitation to See 1

Chapter 2: Understanding Divine Attributes 4

Chapter 3: Reflections of Mercy 7

Chapter 4: The Beauty of Creation 10

Chapter 5: The Power of Wisdom 13

Chapter 6: Manifestations of Justice 16

Chapter 7: The Light of Guidance 20

Chapter 8: Embracing Patience 23

Chapter 9: The Essence of Unity 26

Chapter 10: The Journey Within 29

Chapter 11: The Influence of a Shaykh 32

Chapter 12: Living in Reflection 35

Chapter 13: The Call to Action 38

Chapter 14: A Legacy of Light 41

Chapter 15: Conclusion: The Eternal Connection 44

Dedicated to my beloved shaykh, spiritual father, instructor, guide, mentor, and life coach, Professor Mohammad Abu Laylah of Cairo, Egypt.

Veiled from this world but forever in our hearts.

I am the person I am today because of him...

Chapter 1:

The Invitation to See

The Call to Awareness

The Call to Awareness invites readers into a transformative journey of recognising the divine presence woven into the very fabric of creation. It encourages an awakening to the beauty and intricacy of Allah's attributes, as expressed in the world around us. This call is not limited to a specific group; it transcends boundaries of faith and belief, inviting everyone to pause and reflect on the signs of the Creator manifesting in everyday life.

Each moment offers an opportunity to connect with Allah (SWT) through the lens of His creations, urging us to see beyond the surface and understand the deeper meanings that lie within.

At the heart of this awakening lies the influence of my beloved shaykh, whose teachings serve as a guiding light for many on their spiritual journeys. Through his profound wisdom, he illustrates how the divine attributes of mercy, compassion, and justice are not just abstract concepts but are alive in the world around us. His ability to articulate the relationship between creation and the Creator has inspired countless individuals to seek a closer connection with Allah (SWT). This section will delve into the essence of his teachings, providing readers with a framework to understand their place within this divine tapestry.

As we immerse ourselves in the beauty of creation, we are reminded that Allah (SWT) has adorned the universe with signs that beckon us to notice and appreciate them. The intricate patterns of nature, the resilience of life, and the serenity of the cosmos all reflect divine qualities waiting to be recognised. This call to awareness is not merely an intellectual exercise; it is an invitation to engage our hearts and senses fully. By acknowledging these attributes in our surroundings, we cultivate a deeper sense of gratitude and connection to the world, allowing us to embody these virtues in our daily lives.

To respond to this call, we must cultivate mindfulness and presence. In a world often filled with distractions, the journey towards awareness requires intentionality and an open heart. Simple practices such as observing a sunset, listening to the rustle of leaves, or feeling the warmth of sunlight can awaken us to the divine attributes. Each moment of awareness becomes a prayer, a reflection of our recognition of Allah's (SWT) presence in everything we encounter. This practice not only enriches our spiritual lives but also nurtures a sense of peace and belonging within the vastness of creation.

Ultimately, The Call to Awareness serves as a bridge connecting us to the essence of Allah (SWT) through His divine attributes. As we embrace this journey, we find ourselves transformed, inspired to live in alignment with the virtues we discover in the world around us. Through the teachings of my shaykh and the beauty of creation, we are encouraged to embody these divine qualities, fostering a deeper connection to ourselves, each other, and our Creator. In this shared exploration, we can collectively illuminate our paths, awakening to the profound reality that we are all part of a greater divine narrative.

Embracing the Journey

Embracing the journey of spiritual awakening is a profound invitation to see the world through the lens of divine attributes. It calls upon each of us—Muslim, non-Muslim, or those who identify with no faith—to recognise the beauty and wisdom embedded in creation. As we embark on this path, we are inspired to find Allah's essence reflected in our surroundings, in the people we meet, and in the experiences we encounter. This journey is not merely about observing the world but about engaging deeply with it, allowing the divine light to illuminate our hearts and guide our actions.

The influence of my beloved shaykh serves as a powerful testament to this journey. His teachings encourage us to look beyond the surface, urging us to perceive the divine attributes manifest in every aspect of life. Through his guidance, we learn that kindness, mercy, and compassion are not just ideals but virtues we can embody. By embracing these qualities, we connect with Allah (SWT) on a deeper level, nurturing our souls and fostering a sense of unity with creation. This transformative process invites us to reflect on how our actions resonate with the divine attributes we admire, encouraging us to strive for authenticity in our daily lives.

As we delve into this exploration, we discover that the journey itself holds immense value. Each moment of contemplation, every act of kindness, and the struggles we face are opportunities to connect with Allah's essence. It is through these experiences that we learn resilience, find purpose, and cultivate gratitude. The challenges we encounter are not mere obstacles; they are invitations to deepen our understanding and to grow in our relationship with the divine. In this way, embracing the journey becomes a sacred act, enriching our lives and the lives of those around us.

This journey also emphasises the importance of community and shared experiences. In our quest to embody divine attributes, we find strength and inspiration in one another. Whether through shared prayers, acts of service, or simply engaging in meaningful conversations, we create bonds that reflect the beauty of Allah's creation. By uplifting each other, we cultivate an environment where virtues can flourish, allowing us to collectively embody the essence of divine love and compassion. This interconnectedness reminds us that we are not alone on our journeys; we are part of a greater tapestry woven by the hands of the Creator.

Ultimately, embracing the journey of discovering Allah's essence in creation is a lifelong endeavour filled with richness and depth. It invites us to remain open, curious, and committed to growth. As we reflect on the teachings of my shaykh and strive to embody the virtues illuminated in our experiences, we find ourselves transformed. Each step taken in faith, each moment of grace, brings us closer to our true selves and to Allah (SWT). In this sacred journey, we come to understand that the essence of life lies not just in reaching a destination but in the beauty of the path we walk together.

Chapter 2:

Understanding Divine Attributes

The Essence of Allah's Names

The essence of Allah's names serves as a profound invitation to explore the divine attributes that reflect His presence in creation. Each name of Allah carries a unique significance, encapsulating aspects of His nature that resonate deeply within the human experience. For Muslims, these names are not just titles; they are gateways to understanding the nature of the Divine. For non-Muslims or those without faith, they represent a universal exploration of virtues that transcend religious boundaries. By contemplating these attributes, we can begin to see the interconnectedness of all life and the divine essence that underlies our existence.

As we delve into the names of Allah, we discover that each one invites us to embody its qualities in our daily lives. For instance, the name Al-Rahman (The Most Merciful) encourages us to practice compassion and kindness towards others, while Al-Hakim (The All-Wise) inspires us to seek knowledge and understanding in our actions. These attributes are not confined to religious practice; they are principles that can enrich our interactions and foster a sense of community among diverse individuals. By embracing these qualities, we contribute to a world that mirrors the divine virtues found within the names of Allah.

The beauty of Allah's names is that they resonate with the deepest yearnings of the human soul. Whether one is seeking solace in times of hardship or joy in moments of triumph, these names provide a framework for understanding life's experiences. They remind us that we are not alone in our struggles or triumphs, as the divine presence is woven into the very fabric of our lives. Through reflection on Allah's attributes, we can find comfort and guidance, allowing us to navigate the complexities of existence with grace and resilience.

Moreover, the exploration of Allah's names can foster a sense of unity among all people, regardless of faith. When we recognise the qualities of mercy, justice, and wisdom in ourselves and others, we build bridges of understanding that transcend cultural and religious divides. This shared appreciation of divine attributes can inspire collaborative efforts towards compassion, understanding, and peace in our communities. In a world often marked by division, embracing the essence of Allah's names can serve as a powerful catalyst for collective healing and growth.

Ultimately, the journey to embody the essence of Allah's names is both personal and communal. It challenges us to reflect on our character and aspirations while encouraging us to uplift those around us. Through the teachings of my beloved shaykh, we are reminded that the pursuit of these divine attributes is a lifelong endeavour, one that enriches our souls and connects us to the greater tapestry of creation. In recognising and embodying the essence of Allah's names, we not only illuminate our own paths but also contribute to a brighter, more compassionate world for all.

The Significance of Attributes in Creation

The exploration of Allah's attributes in creation invites us to witness the divine essence that permeates the universe. Each attribute serves as a window into the profound nature of the Creator, allowing us to connect with the divine in a tangible way. When we observe the world around us—the majesty of mountains, the complexity of ecosystems, the intricate design of the human body—we are not merely seeing physical phenomena; we are encountering reflections of Allah's attributes. This perspective transforms our understanding of creation from a series of random occurrences to a cohesive expression of divine qualities, urging us to engage deeply with the world and recognise the signs of Allah's presence in every aspect of life.

As we delve into the significance of these attributes, it becomes clear that they are not just abstract concepts but practical virtues that we can strive to embody. For instance, Allah's attribute of mercy is reflected in the compassion we show towards one another. By embracing this attribute, we not only enhance our relationships with fellow beings but also cultivate a deeper connection with Allah. Each time we act with kindness or seek to alleviate the suffering of others, we participate in the divine narrative of mercy, thereby enriching our spiritual journey. This active engagement encourages us to reflect on how we can mirror these attributes in our daily lives, fostering a community that embodies the essence of divine goodness.

The influence of my beloved shaykh has played a pivotal role in illuminating these connections. His teachings emphasise that recognising Allah's attributes within ourselves and in the world around us can transform our spiritual practice. He encourages us to see beyond the superficial and to understand that every challenge, every joy, and every moment of existence is an opportunity to reflect on these divine qualities. Through his guidance, we learn that embodying Allah's attributes not only elevates our own character but also inspires those around us to embark on their own journeys of self-discovery and spiritual growth.

Moreover, the significance of Allah's attributes extends beyond individual transformation; it has the power to unite diverse communities. In a world often marked by division and misunderstanding, recognising the shared divine qualities within each person can foster empathy and unity. Whether one identifies as Muslim, non-Muslim, or follows no particular faith, the call to embody virtues such as justice, patience, and humility resonates universally. This shared aspiration creates a common ground, where individuals can come together in pursuit of a higher moral standard, reflecting the beauty of Allah's creation through cooperation and mutual respect.

Ultimately, the journey of discovering Allah's attributes within creation is a profound and transformative experience. It invites us to look deeper into the fabric of existence and recognise the divine fingerprints that shape our reality. By embracing these attributes and striving to embody them, we not only enhance our own spiritual lives but also contribute to a more compassionate and understanding world. As we navigate this path, guided by the wisdom of my shaykh, may we find inspiration in the beauty of creation and the divine qualities that dwell within us, illuminating our souls and leading us closer to Allah's essence.

Chapter 3:

Reflections of Mercy

Witnessing Mercy in Nature

Witnessing mercy in nature invites us to open our hearts and minds to the profound manifestations of Allah's attributes that surround us. As we walk through the world, we encounter countless expressions of mercy in the delicate balance of ecosystems, the nurturing of life, and the provision of sustenance. Each morning, the sun rises not only to illuminate our path but also to warm the earth and support the intricate web of life. This daily miracle serves as a reminder of Allah's unfailing mercy, a constant invitation to witness the beauty and compassion that permeates creation.

In the gentle caress of a breeze or the soft rustling of leaves, we find echoes of mercy that invite us to pause and reflect. Nature is a tapestry woven with threads of compassion, each creature playing its role in the grand design. Consider the way a mother bird tirelessly cares for her young, or how flowers bloom even in the harshest conditions, sharing their beauty selflessly. These examples illustrate the essence of mercy that Allah imbues within creation, urging us to recognise our own capacity for kindness and compassion. In observing these moments, we are not merely spectators; we are invited to embody these virtues in our interactions with others.

The oceans embody mercy as they cradle life within their depths, providing sustenance and shelter for countless beings. Each wave that crashes upon the shore carries with it a message of renewal and hope, reminding us that even in the midst of turmoil, there is a promise of calm. This dynamic relationship between the land and sea reflects Allah's infinite mercy, teaching us the importance of balance and resilience. By witnessing this interplay, we gain insights into our own lives, learning to navigate challenges with grace and understanding, much like the tides that ebb and flow.

As we delve deeper into the natural world, we are confronted with the cycles of life and death, a powerful testament to mercy's role in the continuum of existence. The decay of fallen leaves nourishes the soil, allowing new life to flourish. This cycle serves as a profound reminder that mercy often manifests through transformation and renewal. In our own lives, we may encounter moments of hardship and loss, yet it is in these trials that we often find the strength to grow and emerge anew. Embracing this understanding allows us to cultivate patience and acceptance, reflecting the mercy we witness in nature.

Ultimately, witnessing mercy in nature is an invitation to cultivate a deeper connection with Allah's essence. Each moment spent in the embrace of the natural world becomes an opportunity to reflect on our responsibilities as stewards of creation. By recognising the divine attributes at play, we are inspired to embody mercy in our actions, extending compassion to ourselves and those around us. In this way, the beauty of nature not only serves as a reminder of Allah's love and mercy but also as a call to action, urging us to illuminate the world through our own expressions of kindness and grace.

The Role of Compassion in Human Relationships

Compassion stands as one of the most profound attributes that connect human beings, transcending faith, culture, and background. It is the innate ability to empathise with the pain and joy of others, fostering a sense of unity and understanding. When we embrace compassion, we not only acknowledge our shared humanity but also reflect the essence of Allah's mercy. In the context of human relationships, compassion becomes a bridge that links souls, allowing them to experience love, kindness, and support in ways that elevate their shared existence.

In the teachings of Islam, compassion is emphasised as an essential quality that believers should cultivate. The Prophet Muhammad (peace be upon him) demonstrated unparalleled compassion throughout his life, setting a powerful example for all to follow. His interactions with "people" of all walks of life illustrated the transformative power of kindness. By embodying compassion, individuals can create environments where trust and openness thrive, leading to deeper connections. This act of connecting with others not only brings joy and solace but also serves as a reflection of Allah's boundless mercy in the world.

Moreover, compassion challenges us to see beyond our differences and recognise the struggles that others face. In a world that often celebrates division and conflict, the act of extending compassion can be revolutionary. It encourages us to listen deeply, to understand the narratives that shape people's lives, and to respond with kindness rather than judgment. By practising compassion, we nourish relationships that are not only supportive but also transformative, allowing us to grow collectively in our journey towards understanding the divine attributes of Allah.

In the face of adversity, compassion becomes a source of strength. It empowers individuals to rise above personal grievances and to foster an atmosphere of healing and reconciliation.

Each act of compassion, no matter how small, can ignite hope in those who feel lost or alone. This ripple effect can inspire communities to come together, sharing resources and support in ways that uplift everyone involved. When we embody compassion, we invite others to reflect on their own capacity for kindness and generosity, thus encouraging a cycle of positivity that can spread far and wide.

Ultimately, the role of compassion in human relationships is not just about the connections we forge with one another; it is also about our relationship with Allah. By recognising and embodying divine attributes like compassion, we draw closer to the essence of creation and to the Creator Himself. Each compassionate act serves as a reminder of Allah's mercy and love for all of humanity. As we strive to fill our lives with compassion, we illuminate our souls and those of others, creating a legacy of love that transcends time and space, guiding us all toward a deeper understanding of Allah's beautiful essence.

Chapter 4:

The Beauty of Creation

Discovering Aesthetics in the World Around Us

In the journey of life, the world around us is overflowing with beauty and intricacy, inviting us to pause and reflect. Every flower that blooms, every star that twinkles, and every gentle breeze carries within it a reflection of Allah's Divine Attributes. Each element of creation serves as a reminder of His boundless wisdom and artistry. As we engage our senses and open our hearts, we can begin to discover the aesthetics embedded in our surroundings, allowing them to lead us to a deeper understanding of the Creator.

This exploration of beauty is not merely an aesthetic pursuit; it is a spiritual journey that connects us to the essence of Allah (SWT).

Nature, in all its forms, is a canvas painted by the Divine. The mountains stand tall, embodying strength and stability, while rivers flow gracefully, symbolising mercy and sustenance. Each aspect of the natural world offers a glimpse into the attributes of Allah: The Majesty of creation reflects His greatness, while the delicate balance of ecosystems showcases His meticulous design. By observing the harmony that exists in nature, we are invited to appreciate the interconnectedness of life and recognise that every creature, no matter how small, has been endowed with purpose and beauty by the Creator. This realisation can inspire us to cultivate a sense of gratitude and deep respect for the world around us.

Creative visualisation, only when adhering to the sunnah of the Prophet Muhammad (SAW), too, serves as a powerful medium through which we can discover the Divine. Whether through poetry or different types of creativity, the creative expressions of humanity resonate with the attributes of Allah (SWT). Artists, often unknowingly, channel their experiences of beauty, love, and truth into their work, inviting others to share in that experience. This connection can transcend cultural and religious boundaries, uniting individuals in a shared appreciation for the Divine. As we engage with art, we are reminded of our potential to reflect Allah's attributes in our own creativity, encouraging us to express beauty and goodness in our lives.

Our interactions with one another further illuminate the beauty of Allah's creation. In every act of kindness, compassion, and justice, we mirror the Divine attributes of mercy, love, and fairness. Each encounter becomes an opportunity to embody these virtues, allowing the light of Allah (SWT) to shine through us. When we approach others with an open heart and a willingness to see the beauty within them, we foster a sense of community and connection that transcends differences. This communal aspect of discovering beauty reinforces the idea that we are all part of a greater tapestry woven by the Creator, encouraging us to live in a manner that reflects His essence.

Ultimately, discovering the immense beauty in the world around us invites us to embark on a transformative journey. It encourages us to engage with creation not just as observers but as active participants in the reflection of Allah's attributes. By embracing the beauty in nature, art, and humanity, we cultivate a deeper connection with the Divine and inspire those around us to do the same. In this exploration, we find not only inspiration but also a profound responsibility to embody the virtues we recognise in the world. This journey is not an endpoint but a continuous path of enlightenment, guiding us ever closer to the essence of Allah (SWT) in all that surrounds us.

The Creative Spirit in Everyday Life

Every moment of our existence is an invitation to connect with the Divine through the beauty that surrounds us. In the mundane experiences of daily life, we often overlook the intricate manifestations of Allah's attributes. Each sunrise, each rustle of the leaves, and each interaction we have can serve as a reminder of a greater purpose. The creative spirit is not confined to artists or poets; it resides in everyone, waiting to be nurtured and expressed. By cultivating awareness of this creativity, we can begin to see the world through a lens of wonder, recognising that every aspect of creation reflects a facet of the Divine.

Engaging with the creative spirit requires an openness to inspiration that transcends religious boundaries. Whether one identifies as Muslim, non-Muslim, or even as someone without faith, the essence of creativity lies in the act of creation itself. Each individual has the potential to express the Divine attributes of compassion, beauty, and wisdom in their everyday actions. When we approach life with a sense of curiosity and appreciation, we allow ourselves to tap into a wellspring of creativity that connects us to our shared humanity and the Divine essence that we all seek.

As we go about our daily routines, it is essential to cultivate an attitude of gratitude and mindfulness. This can transform ordinary moments into profound experiences of connection with Allah. Simple acts, such as preparing a meal, tending to a garden, or engaging in conversation, can become expressions of our creativity when infused with intention. When we view these activities as opportunities to reflect Allah's attributes, we can find joy and fulfillment in even the smallest tasks. By being present and intentional, we can turn our lives into a canvas where we paint the virtues of love, kindness, and generosity.

The journey toward embodying the creative spirit is not a solitary one. It is enriched by the relationships we build with others. Collaborating with friends, family, or community members can amplify our creativity and inspire us to explore new dimensions of our existence. Sharing ideas, experiences, and perspectives can illuminate different aspects of Allah's qualities, reminding us that we are all interconnected. In this way, the act of creating becomes a communal experience that nurtures our souls and fosters a deeper understanding of the divine.

Ultimately, embracing the creative spirit in our everyday lives is a path to spiritual awakening. It invites us to recognise the sacredness in all that we do and to see the divine presence in the world around us. By engaging with the beauty of creation and embodying Allah's attributes, we can cultivate a deeper connection with ourselves, each other, and the Creator. This journey is a testament to the profound influence of spiritual guidance, encouraging us to not only appreciate the brilliance of creation but also to reflect that brilliance in our own lives.

Chapter 5:

The Power of Wisdom

Learning from Life's Challenges

Life is full of challenges that test our resilience and build our character. Each obstacle presents an opportunity for growth, reflection, and a deeper understanding of ourselves and our relationship with the Divine. In moments of hardship, when the weight of the world seems unbearable, we are often compelled to seek solace and guidance beyond our immediate circumstances. This quest for meaning in suffering can lead us to the realisation that challenges are not merely burdens to bear but profound lessons meant to illuminate our path toward Allah's essence.

The trials we face can be seen as mirrors reflecting our inner state and our connection to Allah (SWT). Just as a polished gem shines brighter under pressure, our souls are refined through adversity. Each challenge becomes a unique invitation to recognise and embody the Divine attributes that Allah has instilled within us. Patience, resilience, compassion, and gratitude are virtues that often emerge in the face of difficulty, allowing us to connect with Allah's essence more deeply. By embracing these moments, we cultivate a spirit that resonates with our Creator's attributes, allowing us to witness His presence in our lives.

Moreover, learning from life's challenges fosters empathy and compassion for others. Those who have faced trials are often more understanding of the struggles that others endure. When we reflect on our experiences, we realise that every hardship we have faced connects us to the broader tapestry of humanity. This understanding encourages us to support one another, creating a community that embodies the virtues of mercy and kindness. By recognising Allah's hand in our challenges, we can inspire others to find their own strength and resilience, fostering a sense of unity that transcends faith and belief.

The teachings of my beloved shaykh serve as a guiding light during these turbulent times. His wisdom reminds us that every challenge is a step on the path toward spiritual enlightenment and cleansing. He encouraged his followers to view obstacles as opportunities for reflection and growth, urging us to seek Allah's pleasure amidst our struggles. By embodying the qualities of steadfastness and faith, we can transform our trials into stepping stones that lead us closer to our Creator. His teachings inspire us to not only endure difficulties but to thrive through them, illuminating the path for others who may be lost in their own darkness.

Ultimately, learning from life's challenges is a profound journey that invites us to connect with Allah through His divine attributes. Each experience, whether joyful or painful, serves a purpose in our spiritual development. As we navigate the complexities of life, let us remain open to the lessons that await us. In doing so, we can cultivate a deeper relationship with Allah (SWT), embodying the virtues that reflect His essence and sharing that light with the world around us. Embracing challenges as opportunities for growth not only transforms our own lives but also empowers us to illuminate the paths of others, creating a ripple effect of faith, hope, and love.

The Role of Intellect in Faith

The intellect plays a pivotal role in the journey of faith, serving as both a guide and a bridge to the divine. In a world filled with distractions and uncertainties, the ability to think critically and reflect deeply becomes a pathway to understanding Allah's essence as manifested in creation. When we engage our intellect, we embark on a quest to explore the intricate tapestry of life, where every thread offers a glimpse of Allah's attributes. This exploration encourages us to ponder the beauty and complexity of the universe, fostering a sense of awe and reverence that strengthens our connection with the Creator.

Intellectual engagement allows individuals to grapple with profound questions about existence and purpose. The pursuit of knowledge is not merely an academic endeavour; it is deeply spiritual. Every inquiry into the mysteries of life can lead to an appreciation of Allah's wisdom and mercy. By contemplating the natural world, from the majestic mountains to the delicate flowers, one can begin to see reflections of Divine qualities such as power, creativity, and sustenance. This process invites both Muslims and non-Muslims alike to recognise the signs of Allah in their surroundings, offering a universal message that transcends religious boundaries.

Moreover, the intellect helps to dispel doubts and misconceptions that may cloud one's faith journey. Engaging critically with religious texts and teachings allows for a more profound and personal understanding of spiritual truths. It encourages believers to ask questions and seek answers, thereby cultivating a deeper relationship with Allah. This active engagement fosters a sense of ownership over one's faith, transforming it from mere tradition into a living, breathing experience. As individuals navigate their spiritual paths, the intellect acts as a companion, illuminating the way and encouraging them to embody the virtues of Allah in their daily lives.

The interplay between intellect and faith is particularly evident in the teachings of my beloved shaykh, who emphasised the importance of understanding Allah's attributes through both the heart and the mind. His approach inspired countless individuals to delve into the depths of their beliefs, urging them to seek knowledge not only for personal growth but as a means to serve others. By embodying divine attributes such as compassion, justice, and humility, individuals can reflect the essence of Allah in their actions, creating ripples of positive change within their communities. This embodiment of virtues is a testament to the transformative power of faith when coupled with intellectual exploration.

In conclusion, the role of intellect in faith is not merely about acquiring knowledge; it is a profound journey towards understanding the Divine. By engaging with the world around us through thoughtful reflection and inquiry, we can uncover the beauty of Allah's attributes in creation. This journey invites everyone—Muslims, non-Muslims, and those seeking a deeper connection with the universe—to explore their beliefs and discover the essence of Allah in their lives. Through this shared quest for knowledge and understanding, we can inspire one another to embody and reflect the divine virtues that make our existence meaningful.

Chapter 6:

Manifestations of Justice

Justice in Nature's Balance

In every corner of the natural world, we witness the profound expression of justice that resonates with Allah's attributes. From the intricate ecosystems that sustain life to the delicate balance of day and night, nature serves as a living testament to the divine order established by the Creator. Each element, from the smallest insect to the mightiest mountain, plays a vital role in maintaining harmony, illustrating that justice is not merely a human concept but a fundamental principle embedded in the fabric of existence. By observing these patterns, we can deepen our understanding of Allah's essence, recognising how His attributes manifest in every aspect of creation.

To connect with Allah through His attributes is to embark on a journey of self-discovery and personal transformation. Each time we engage with the Divine, whether through prayer, reflection, or acts of kindness, we open our hearts to the possibility of change.

This process invites us to shed layers of ego and fear, allowing the light of Divine attributes to shine through us. As we strive to emulate these qualities, we begin to experience profound shifts in our relationships, as well as our understanding of ourselves and others. The invitation to see becomes an opportunity for growth, fostering a community rooted in love and understanding.

As we delve deeper into the essence of creation, we find that the transformative power of Divine attributes extends beyond personal development; it impacts our collective existence. When individuals embody these virtues, they cultivate an environment where love, justice, and compassion flourish. This transformation ripples outwards, encouraging others to engage with their own spiritual journeys. By recognising the Divine in each other, regardless of faith or belief, we create a tapestry of unity that transcends superficial differences, inviting everyone to participate in the divine dance of life.

Ultimately, the journey of embodying Allah's attributes is one of continuous learning and deepening connection. It challenges us to look beyond the surface and to embrace the diversity of creation as a reflection of the Divine's multifaceted nature. By embracing this transformative power, we not only enrich our own lives but also contribute to the collective awakening of humanity. In this illumination, we find the essence of love and compassion that binds us all, creating a world that echoes the beauty of Allah's attributes and inspires each of us to shine brightly in our unique ways.

The beauty of justice in nature is evident in the way species coexist, each fulfilling its purpose without infringing upon another. Predators and prey, plants and animals, all engage in a dance of interdependence, ensuring that life continues to flourish. This cyclical relationship teaches us the importance of respecting boundaries and embracing our roles within the greater scheme of life. As we reflect on this balance, we are reminded of the Qur'anic teachings that emphasise fairness and equity. Allah's creation beckons us to emulate these qualities, urging us to practice justice in our interactions with others and to advocate for the rights of all beings.

Moreover, nature's balance extends beyond mere survival; it embodies a profound sense of mercy and compassion. The changing seasons illustrate how loss can lead to renewal, just as Allah's mercy envelops all of creation, offering solace during times of hardship. Each spring brings forth new life, symbolising hope and the guarantee of renewal. This cycle encourages us to embrace forgiveness and understanding in our lives, reflecting the Divine attributes of compassion and mercy. By aligning ourselves with nature's rhythms, we can cultivate a deeper connection with Allah, fostering a spirit of gratitude for the myriad blessings that surround us.

Justice in nature also serves as a reminder of accountability. Just as every element of creation has a purpose, we too are called to fulfill our responsibilities. The natural world operates on principles of cause and effect, where actions yield consequences. This mirrors the teachings of our faith, which emphasise that every deed, whether good or bad, will be accounted for. By acknowledging this relationship, we are inspired to act with intention and integrity, striving to embody the Divine virtues that shape our character. In this way, we become active participants in the balance of justice, contributing positively to our communities and the world at large.

Ultimately, "Justice in Nature's Balance" invites readers to engage with the profound lessons that Allah imparts through creation. By recognising the intricate interplay of justice, mercy, and accountability in the natural world, we can cultivate a deeper awareness of our place within it. As we strive to embody these divine attributes, we not only enhance our personal journeys but also illuminate the path for others. Through this collective effort, we can honour the essence of Allah, fostering a world where justice prevails and every soul is uplifted in the light of His mercy and love.

Striving for Fairness in Society

Striving for fairness in society is an endeavour that transcends cultural, religious, and philosophical boundaries, uniting humanity in its quest for justice and equity. Fairness is a reflection of Allah's divine attribute of Al-Adl, the Just. To embody this trait is to recognise the inherent dignity of every individual, regardless of their background or beliefs. In our daily lives, we are called to mirror this Divine quality, ensuring that our actions promote equality and compassion. Whether we are engaging in community service, advocating for the marginalised, or simply treating others with kindness, each act of fairness is a step toward fulfilling our spiritual potential and honour

ing Allah's essence in creation.

In the pursuit of fairness, we must first cultivate a deep understanding of the world around us. This involves listening to the stories of others, especially those whose voices have been historically silenced. By embracing empathy, we allow ourselves to connect with the struggles and triumphs of our fellow beings. This connection not only enriches our perspective but also deepens our relationship with Allah, as we recognise that every individual is a manifestation of His creation. In this way, striving for fairness becomes an act of worship, a means of drawing closer to Allah by honouring the diversity He has instilled in the world.

Moreover, striving for fairness is inherently linked to the principles of accountability and responsibility. As stewards of the earth, we bear the duty to challenge injustices and inequities that permeate our societies. This may require us to confront uncomfortable truths about our own privileges and biases. Embracing fairness means taking a stand against oppression and advocating for those who cannot advocate for themselves. It calls us to engage in discourse that fosters understanding, rather than division, and to create spaces where all voices can be heard. In doing so, we reflect the divine attribute of Al- Hakam, the Judge, who sees beyond appearances and understands the true essence of justice.

Education plays a pivotal role in fostering a fair society. It empowers individuals to question societal norms and to seek out knowledge that promotes understanding and justice. By encouraging critical thinking and compassion in our educational institutions, we lay the groundwork for future generations to champion fairness. This commitment to education is a reflection of Allah's wisdom, as He encourages us to seek knowledge and understanding. When we prioritise equitable access to education for all, we are not only uplifting individuals but also strengthening the fabric of our communities, ensuring that everyone has the opportunity to thrive.

Ultimately, striving for fairness is a journey that invites us to reflect on our own actions and intentions. It challenges us to embody the divine attributes of Allah in our interactions with others and to create a world where justice prevails. Whether through small acts of kindness, community engagement, or advocacy for systemic change, each effort contributes to a greater tapestry of fairness. As we illuminate our paths with the light of Allah's essence, we find that the pursuit of fairness is not just a goal but a sacred responsibility, one that enriches our souls and draws us closer to the divine.

Chapter 7:

The Light of Guidance

Seeking Direction in Daily Choices

In the journey of life, each decision we face presents an opportunity to connect with the essence of creation. Seeking direction in our daily choices can often feel overwhelming, yet it is crucial to recognise that even the smallest actions can reflect the Divine attributes of Allah (SWT). Whether we are Muslims, non-Muslims, or individuals without faith, the principles of kindness, patience, and compassion resonate universally. By aligning our choices with these virtues, we can transform our daily lives into a canvas that showcases the beauty of Allah's essence.

Every moment offers a chance to reflect on how our decisions align with the divine attributes we admire. For instance, when faced with challenges, we can embody patience—Sabr—allowing us to navigate difficulties with grace and resilience. This approach not only serves our personal growth but also influences those around us. As we strive to display these qualities, we invite others to witness the light of Allah's attributes in action. It is through our reflection of these virtues that we create a ripple effect, inspiring others to seek the same illumination in their lives.

Furthermore, understanding that our choices can be a form of worship elevates the mundane to the sacred. Each act of kindness, whether a smile shared with a stranger or a helping hand offered to those in need, becomes a means of connecting with Allah (SWT). In choosing to embody love and compassion, we actively participate in a divine dialogue with the world around us. This perspective can be transformative, encouraging us to seek the deeper meaning behind our actions and to recognise the significance of our everyday interactions.

In moments of uncertainty, we can take solace in the idea that Allah's attributes serve as guiding lights. When faced with decisions, reflecting on the qualities we wish to embody—such as mercy, justice, and humility—can illuminate our path. This practice encourages mindfulness and intentionality, reminding us that our choices are not merely reactions but opportunities for growth and connection. As we cultivate this awareness, we become more attuned to the divine presence in our lives, finding clarity in the chaos that often surrounds us.

Ultimately, seeking direction in our daily choices is about fostering a deeper relationship with Allah (SWT) and recognising the beauty of His attributes in ourselves and others.

This journey invites us to engage with our surroundings through a lens of gratitude and compassion, enhancing our spiritual experience. As we strive to embody these virtues, we not only enrich our own lives but also contribute to a world that reflects the Divine essence of creation. Through our choices, we can illuminate the path for ourselves and others, creating a legacy that honours the profound influence of our beloved shaykh and the timeless truth of Allah's attributes.

The Impact of Spiritual Guidance

The essence of spiritual guidance lies in its ability to illuminate the path toward deeper understanding and connection with the Divine. Through the teachings of my shaykh, we are invited to perceive the world around us as a reflection of Allah's beautiful attributes. This perspective encourages us to recognise the Divine presence in everyday life, fostering a sense of reverence and gratitude. Such guidance serves not only to inspire introspection but also to cultivate an appreciation for the interconnectedness of all creation, reminding us that every facet of life is imbued with spiritual significance.

My shaykh's wisdom resonates deeply with individuals from all walks of life, transcending cultural and religious boundaries. By emphasising the importance of seeing Allah's attributes in nature, relationships, and personal experiences, the teachings provide a universal platform for understanding and growth. This inclusivity allows both Muslims and non-Muslims, as well as those seeking faith, to find common ground in the pursuit of truth and beauty. The transformative power of spiritual guidance lies in its ability to unify diverse souls, urging them to reflect on their own virtues and strive for a higher state of being.

As we explore Allah's attributes through the lens of my shaykh's teachings, we uncover the profound impact these qualities can have on our personal lives. For instance, embodying the attribute of mercy can lead to more compassionate interactions with others, while embracing wisdom can enhance our decision-making processes. By striving to reflect these Divine characteristics, we not only enrich our own lives but also contribute positively to the world around us. This journey of self-improvement is a testament to the transformative power of spiritual guidance, as it empowers us to align our actions with our higher purpose.

Moreover, the influence of my shaykh extends beyond individual transformation; it acts as a catalyst for collective change within communities. When individuals embrace spiritual guidance and embody Divine attributes, the ripple effect can lead to a more harmonious society. The teachings encourage collaboration, understanding, and empathy among people, fostering an environment where love and respect thrive. In this way, spiritual guidance not only nurtures the soul but also cultivates a sense of responsibility toward others, inspiring a collective awakening to the beauty inherent in our shared humanity.

Ultimately, the impact of spiritual guidance is profound and far-reaching. It invites us to embark on a journey of self-discovery, urging us to see the Divine essence within ourselves and others. Through the teachings of my shaykh, we are reminded that by connecting with Allah's attributes, we can experience a deeper sense of purpose and fulfillment. This journey is not merely about personal growth; it is about illuminating the world with the light of divine virtues, creating a legacy of love and understanding that transcends time and space. Embracing this guidance, we can aspire to become beacons of light, reflecting Allah's attributes in all that we do.

Chapter 8:

Embracing Patience

The Lessons of Time and Endurance

The passage of time is an unyielding teacher, imparting wisdom through its trials and tribulations. As we navigate the journey of life, we encounter moments that challenge our resolve and test our patience. In these instances, we learn the importance of endurance, a quality that reflects Allah's Divine attributes. Just as Allah is Ever-Present and All-Knowing, we are invited to embrace our experiences and grow from them, finding strength in the face of adversity. The lessons of time and endurance remind us that every moment is an opportunity for reflection, growth, and a deeper connection with the Divine.

In the natural world, we see the embodiment of endurance in the changing seasons. Winter's harshness gives way to the bloom of spring, illustrating the cycle of life and renewal. Each season teaches us patience; the trees shed their leaves not in despair but in preparation for new growth. Similarly, as we endure the hardships of life, we are reminded that these challenges are often precursors to our own blossoming. This realisation fosters a sense of hope in our hearts, encouraging us to look for the beauty that lies beyond our struggles, ultimately guiding us back to Allah's essence in creation.

The stories of prophets and saints throughout history serve as powerful examples of endurance in the face of trials. Their unwavering faith and determination inspire us to persevere, regardless of our circumstances. Each narrative is a testament to the strength of the human spirit when aligned with Divine purpose. By reflecting on their journeys, we can draw parallels to our own lives and recognise that our struggles are not in vain; they are a part of a larger tapestry woven by Allah's hand. This understanding deepens our connection with the Divine, encouraging us to embody the attributes of patience and resilience in our daily lives.

As we cultivate the virtue of endurance, we also learn to appreciate the beauty of time itself. It is through the passage of time that we gain perspective, allowing us to see the larger picture of our existence. Moments of joy and sorrow are intertwined, shaping us into individuals capable of experiencing a wide range of emotions. This rich emotional tapestry is a reflection of Allah's infinite wisdom, reminding us that every phase of life serves a purpose.

By embracing the lessons of time, we grow closer to understanding Allah's attributes—His Mercy, Compassion, and Ultimate Wisdom.

Ultimately, the lessons of time and endurance invite us to foster a spirit of gratitude. Each challenge we face becomes a stepping stone toward greater understanding and connection with Allah. We learn to view life's trials not as burdens, but as opportunities to embody the virtues Allah cherishes. This perspective transforms our experiences into profound teachings, guiding us to live in alignment with the divine attributes we see reflected in creation. As we navigate our paths, we become illuminated souls, striving to mirror Allah's essence in our actions and interactions with the world around us.

Cultivating Inner Peace

Cultivating inner peace is a journey that transcends faith boundaries, inviting everyone—Muslims, non-Muslims, and those who identify with no particular belief—to explore the divine attributes of Allah reflected in the world around us. This exploration can lead to a profound sense of tranquillity and connection, allowing individuals to find solace in the chaos of life. Inner peace is not merely the absence of turmoil; it is the presence of a deep-seated serenity that arises when we align ourselves with the Divine virtues inherent in creation. By embracing the qualities of mercy, compassion, and wisdom, we can create a harmonious existence that resonates with our true selves.

To cultivate this inner peace, one must first embark on a path of self-awareness. This involves recognising the attributes of Allah that manifest in everyday life, from the beauty of nature to the kindness of strangers. Each moment serves as a reminder of these divine qualities, urging us to reflect on our own actions and attitudes. In doing so, we can begin to embody the virtues we admire, fostering a sense of harmony within ourselves. This self-awareness is a crucial step in the journey; it invites us to pause, reflect, and reconnect with our inner selves, paving the way for deeper spiritual growth.

Praying, meditation, and mindfulness can be powerful aids in this journey. By setting aside time to calm our minds and concentrate on our breathing, we open a space for Divine qualities to grow within us. These moments of tranquillity help us to hear the gentle prompts of our hearts and the guidance of Allah's essence in our lives. As we engage in these practices, we build a wellspring of peace that supports us through life's difficulties. Being present allows us to recognise the beauty of creation, reminding us of our connectedness and the Divine spark that exists in each of us.

Additionally, fostering a sense of gratitude can significantly enhance our inner peace. When we focus on the blessings in our lives, we shift our perspective from one of shortage to abundance. Recognising the gifts that Allah has bestowed upon us—whether they are the love of family, the beauty of nature, or the simple joy of a shared smile— encourages a deeper connection to the Divine. This gratitude can transform our outlook, allowing us to respond to life's difficulties with grace and resilience, ultimately leading to a more peaceful existence.

In conclusion, cultivating inner peace is a transformative journey that invites each of us to connect with Allah's Divine attributes in our own unique way. By embracing self-awareness, praying, reading the Quran, practising mindfulness, and nurturing gratitude, we can embody the virtues reflected in creation. This journey is not only a personal endeavour but also a communal one, fostering connections that transcend differences and unite us in our shared humanity. As we strive to illuminate our souls with the essence of Allah, we create a ripple effect, inspiring others to seek their own paths toward understanding, peace and harmony.

Chapter 9:

The Essence of Unity

Understanding Interconnectedness

In the intricate tapestry of existence, everything is woven together—an intricate network of life that reflects the essence of Allah (SWT). To grasp the concept of interconnectedness is to recognise that every element of creation serves as a mirror, revealing Divine attributes that guide us toward a deeper understanding of our Creator. When we look around, we see not just individual entities, but a harmonious symphony where each note, each being, contributes to a greater purpose. This realisation encourages us to embrace the idea that our lives are interconnected, urging us to nurture relationships based on compassion, empathy, and understanding.

As we delve into the beauty of interconnectedness, we must acknowledge that each attribute of Allah (SWT) is manifested throughout creation. The vastness of the universe, the delicate balance of ecosystems, and the profound complexity of human body and emotions all point to the Divine qualities of wisdom, mercy, and unity. In recognising these attributes in the world around us, we are invited to cultivate a relationship with Allah that transcends rituals and dogmas, allowing us to see His presence in every moment and every interaction. This perspective invites not only Muslims but all people, regardless of their beliefs, to engage with the Divine through the lens of creation.

The teachings of my beloved shaykh illuminate this path, emphasising that our understanding of interconnectedness can be transformative. It is through this lens that we can see our responsibilities toward one another and the world we inhabit. My shaykh's profound insights urge us to reflect on how we can embody the divine attributes of compassion and generosity. When we recognise that our actions ripple through the interconnected web of life, we begin to act with intention and mindfulness, striving to leave a positive impact on those around us.

Moreover, interconnectedness invites us to engage in a profound dialogue with creation itself. Every interaction is an opportunity to reflect Allah's attributes, whether it's through a simple act of kindness or a moment of deep understanding. By acknowledging our place within this Divine framework, we cultivate a sense of gratitude that resonates with the essence of our existence. This gratitude fosters a deeper connection with Allah (SWT) and encourages us to live in harmony with each other and the world. It is a call to action, inspiring us to be agents of positive change, not just for ourselves, but for the collective good.

Ultimately, understanding interconnectedness is a personal journey that enriches our spiritual lives and enhances our relationships with others. As we learn to see the Divine attributes in creation, we become more attuned to our own virtues, striving to embody them in our daily lives. It is through this embodiment that we forge a deeper connection with Allah (SWT) and contribute to the greater good of humanity. The journey toward understanding interconnectedness isn't merely an intellectual exercise; it is a heartfelt invitation to experience the beauty and unity of creation, leading us closer to the essence of Allah in all that we do.

Building Bridges Across Divides

In a world frequently characterised by division, misunderstandings, intolerance, and greed, the effort to create connections across divides is not merely an ideal; it is an essential necessity. The essence of Allah (SWT) encourages us to appreciate the diversity of creation and to look beyond our differences. Each individual, regardless of their faith or beliefs, holds within them a spark of the Divine. By acknowledging this common essence, we can cultivate compassion, empathy, and understanding among one another. The beauty of Allah's attributes—His Mercy, Kindness, and Wisdom—guides us to interact in ways that go beyond superficial barriers.

The teachings of my beloved shaykh illuminate this path, showing us how to reflect Allah's attributes in our interactions. He emphasised that every encounter is an opportunity to practice these virtues. When we approach one another with an open heart, we can often find common ground, even where we initially see differences. The act of listening, of truly hearing another's story, allows us to appreciate the myriad ways in which Allah's creation expresses itself. This active engagement nurtures a sense of belonging and connection, cultivating a community that celebrates diversity while remaining united in our shared humanity.

Embodying the virtues of Allah requires intentionality and effort. As we strive to mirror His attributes, we begin to understand the transformative power of love and acceptance. Each act of kindness we extend has the potential to dissolve barriers, creating ripples of harmony that extend far beyond our immediate surroundings. The stories of individuals who have embraced this path serve as powerful reminders of what is possible when we choose to build bridges instead of walls. By sharing these narratives, we not only inspire ourselves but also encourage others to partake in this sacred journey toward unity.

Challenges will inevitably arise as we endeavour to connect across divides.

Misunderstandings, prejudices, and historical grievances can cloud our perceptions and hinder our efforts. However, the teachings of my shaykh remind us that resilience is rooted in faith. It is through sincere dialogue and mutual respect that we can navigate these obstacles. By invoking Allah's guidance, we can approach contentious issues with a spirit of humility, seeking to understand rather than to be understood. This approach not only enriches our own spiritual journey but also contributes to a larger narrative of peace and reconciliation.

In the pursuit of building bridges, let us remember the profound impact of our actions and words. Each one of us carries the responsibility to reflect Allah's beautiful attributes in our lives. As we embark on this journey together, we must remain vigilant in our commitment to empathy and understanding. By doing so, we can transform our communities and, ultimately, the world around us. In illuminating the essence of Allah through our connections with others, we not only honour our Creator but also fulfil our purpose as stewards of His creation, fostering a legacy of unity that spans across all divides.

Chapter 10:

The Journey Within

Reflecting on Personal Experiences

Reflecting on personal experiences can be a profound journey that invites us to see the world through a lens of Divine beauty. Each moment in our lives, from the mundane to the extraordinary, serves as a canvas painted with the colours of Allah's attributes. These experiences, when examined closely, reveal how creation mirrors the essence of the Creator. In the quiet moments of reflection, whether one identifies as a Muslim, a non-Muslim, or someone exploring spirituality, the opportunity to connect with Allah (SWT) becomes accessible. It is in this reflective space that we can uncover the guiding light within us, illuminating the path towards embodying divine virtues.

As we engage with our personal narratives, we often encounter challenges that test our resilience and compassion. These trials are not merely obstacles; they are moments of growth that allow us to experience Allah's attributes of mercy and wisdom. For instance, in times of hardship, we may find ourselves leaning on the strength of our faith or the support of our community. This reliance is a manifestation of Allah's strength and compassion, reminding us that we are never alone. It is through these struggles that we learn to cultivate patience, gratitude, and understanding, virtues that resonate deeply with the divine qualities we seek to embody.

Moreover, the beauty of creation itself serves as a constant reminder of Allah's presence in our lives. A sunset, a blooming flower, or the laughter of a child can evoke feelings of awe and wonder, drawing our attention to the meticulous craftsmanship of the Creator. These moments invite us to pause and reflect on the Divine attributes represented in the world around us. By taking the time to appreciate the intricacies of creation, we can deepen our connection with Allah (SWT) and recognise that His essence is woven into the fabric of our daily existence. It is an invitation to see beyond the surface and appreciate the profound reflections of divinity in our surroundings.

In sharing our experiences with others, we foster a sense of community and understanding. Each story becomes a thread in the larger tapestry of human experience, weaving together diverse perspectives and insights. This sharing is not limited to those of the same faith; it transcends boundaries, reaching out to anyone open to exploring the Divine. By articulating our personal journeys, we encourage others to embark on their own path of reflection, ultimately leading to a broader appreciation of Allah's attributes and the interconnectedness of all creation. In this space of shared wisdom, we can inspire one another to live with intention and purpose.

Ultimately, reflecting on personal experiences is a transformative process that allows us to encounter Allah's essence in a deeply personal way. It empowers us to recognise the Divine attributes in ourselves and in others, urging us to embody these virtues in our interactions and daily lives. This journey is not solely for those who identify with a particular faith; it is an invitation for everyone to explore the depths of their own experiences and the profound beauty that lies within. As we reflect, we become beacons of light, guiding others towards a greater understanding of the Divine and inspiring them to live in harmony with Allah's beautiful attributes.

Embodying Divine Attributes in Daily Life

Embodying Divine attributes in daily life invites us to reflect on the essence of Allah's attributes and how they manifest in our everyday existence. By recognising these attributes within creation, we begin to understand our connection to the Divine. Each moment offers us an opportunity to witness kindness, mercy, justice, and beauty, not only in the world around us but also within ourselves. The journey of embodying these qualities transforms our interactions, elevating our relationships and deepening our spiritual connection. Whether one identifies as a Muslim, a seeker of truth, or simply a curious soul, this invitation to see and embody the divine serves as a pathway to a more harmonious and fulfilling life.

To embody Divine attributes, we must first cultivate awareness. This means looking beyond the surface of daily encounters and recognising the sacredness inherent in each moment. When we see a stranger's smile or hear a child's laughter, we are reminded of Allah's mercy and joy. By consciously acknowledging these moments, we align ourselves with the essence of Divine qualities, allowing them to inspire our actions. The teachings of my beloved shaykh guide us in this practice, encouraging us to embrace a mindset of gratitude and appreciation. Each experience becomes a reflection of Allah's wisdom, challenging us to respond with compassion and understanding.

The practice of embodying Divine attributes also extends to our interactions with others. How we treat those around us serves as a mirror of our spiritual state. When we approach others with love, patience, and respect, we model the attributes of Allah, demonstrating the importance of community and connection. In this way, our actions can become a source of inspiration for others and a source of devotion for the Divine. My shaykh often emphasised the significance of serving humanity as a means of drawing closer to the Divine. This service not only elevates our spirit but also cultivates a sense of unity among all of creation, reminding us that we are all interconnected.

Moreover, embodying Divine attributes requires a commitment to personal growth and self-reflection. It involves recognising our shortcomings and striving to improve ourselves in alignment with Allah's qualities. The journey is not one without challenges; it requires continuous effort and a humble, forgiving heart. My shaykh taught that true transformation occurs when we seek to embody these attributes not just in moments of ease but also during trials. By facing difficulties with resilience and grace, we mirror Allah's strength and wisdom, allowing our character to shine even in adversity.

Ultimately, embodying divine attributes is a lifelong endeavour that enriches our spiritual journey. As we strive to reflect Allah's essence in our lives, we become beacons of light for ourselves and others. The call to embody these virtues transcends religious boundaries, inviting all individuals to participate in a collective movement toward love, compassion, and understanding. Through the teachings of my shaykh, we are reminded that every act of kindness, every moment of patience, and every expression of gratitude is a step closer to realising the Divine potential within us all. In doing so, we not only enhance our own lives but also contribute to a more compassionate and harmonious world.

Chapter 11:

The Influence of a Shaykh

Personal Stories of Transformation

Throughout our journeys, we often encounter moments that spark profound change, illuminating the path toward a deeper connection with the Divine. One such story is that of a young woman who, disillusioned by life's challenges, found herself at a crossroads. Her search for meaning led her to a humble gathering led by my shaykh. It was there, amidst the warmth of community and the wisdom shared, that she began to perceive Allah's attributes in the resilience of those around her. Through their struggles and triumphs, she saw patience, compassion, and strength mirrored in their stories, igniting a desire within her to embody these virtues in her own life.

Another powerful testament comes from the life of a man who had long wrestled with anger and frustration. Years of hardship left him feeling disconnected from the world and from Allah. After meeting my shaykh, he began to recognise mercy and forgiveness not only as qualities to be admired but as essential traits to cultivate within himself. Guided by my shaykh's insights, he learnt to channel his experiences into acts of kindness, transforming his anger into a source of motivation. This transformation didn't just change his perspective; it altered the way he interacted with his family and the community, bridging gaps and fostering unity where there was once discord.

Another woman's path serves as a powerful example of transformation through understanding Allah's attributes. A gifted individual, she struggled to express herself amid societal expectations and personal insecurities. As she started to explore the concept of beauty as an attribute of Allah, her artistic expression took on new meaning. My shaykh encouraged her to see her creativity as a reflection of the Divine, allowing her to embrace vulnerability and authenticity in her work. Whilst on the journey of her soul, she came to realise that her talents were not solely for her own fulfillment; it became a means for others to connect with their own experiences of beauty and grace. By embracing her gifts, she not only transformed her own life but also inspired many others to discover their own expressions of love and creativity.

Then there's the story of a businessman who found himself entrenched in a world driven by profit and competition. The relentless pursuit of success left him feeling empty and spiritually unfulfilled. After engaging with my shaykh's teachings on generosity as a Divine attribute, he began to reevaluate his priorities. He started initiatives that aimed to uplift the marginalised in his community, recognising that true success lies in the impact one has on others. This shift not only revitalised his spirit but also fostered a culture of compassion and collaboration within his business, demonstrating how embodying Divine attributes can create a ripple effect of positive change.

These personal stories of transformation serve as powerful reminders that the journey to connect with Allah and embody His attributes is deeply personal yet universal. Each individual's path reflects the myriad ways in which we can seek and experience the Divine in our lives. Through the lessons imparted by my shaykh, we are invited to recognise that our struggles, triumphs, and transformations are threads in the intricate tapestry of creation, all woven together by the essence of Allah's beautiful attributes. As we share these narratives, may they inspire readers from all walks of life to embark on their own journeys of self-discovery and spiritual awakening, realising they too can illuminate their souls through a deeper understanding of the Divine.

The Role of Mentorship in Spiritual Growth

Mentorship plays a crucial role in spiritual growth, serving as a bridge between the seeker and the Divine. In the journey of connecting with Allah (SWT) through His attributes, a mentor acts as a guiding light, revealing the profound wisdom embedded in creation. This relationship transcends mere instruction, fostering a deep emotional and spiritual connection that inspires individuals to reflect upon the essence of their existence. Through the lens of mentorship, seekers can uncover the beauty of Allah's attributes, seeing them mirrored in themselves and the world around them.

A mentor, particularly one who embodies the virtues of Allah like my beloved shaykh, offers invaluable insights into the complexities of life and spirituality. This relationship allows for a personal exploration of faith, where questions can be posed without fear and wisdom is shared generously. As seekers observe their mentors in action (like that of me and my shaykh), they learn to cultivate qualities such as compassion, patience, and love— attributes that resonate with the Divine essence. This transformative experience encourages individuals from all walks of life to embrace their spiritual journey, fostering a sense of belonging within a larger community of seekers.

The influence of a mentor extends beyond direct teachings; it permeates the very fabric of a seeker's life. By witnessing the mentor's devotion and sincerity, students are inspired to deepen their own relationship with Allah (SWT). This dynamic not only nurtures spiritual growth but also instils a desire to reflect divine attributes in everyday interactions. The mentor's role becomes a catalyst, igniting a passion for seeking knowledge and understanding the world through a spiritual lens. This process encourages individuals to embody the virtues they admire, thus creating a ripple effect of goodness and compassion in their surroundings.

Moreover, mentorship fosters resilience in the face of life's challenges. A mentor provides not just guidance, but also support during times of doubt and difficulty. This relationship helps seekers navigate their spiritual path with confidence, reminding them that struggles are an integral part of the journey. Through encouragement and shared experiences, mentors instill a sense of hope and perseverance, allowing individuals to see beyond their immediate circumstances and recognise the Divine purpose in every trial. Such resilience is essential for anyone striving to connect with Allah and embody His attributes in a world that often feels overwhelming.

Ultimately, the role of mentorship in spiritual growth is to illuminate the path towards understanding and embodying Allah's essence. It creates a nurturing environment where seekers can thrive, encouraging them to see the Divine in creation and in themselves. As individuals engage with their mentors, they are invited to not only learn but also to grow, transforming their spiritual journey into a lifelong commitment to embodying the beautiful attributes of Allah (SWT). This powerful dynamic not only enriches the lives of the mentees but also enhances the mentor's own spiritual journey, creating a shared experience of enlightenment that transcends all boundaries.

Chapter 12:

Living in Reflection

Practical Steps to Embody Divine Attributes

To truly embody the Divine attributes of Allah, one must first cultivate awareness and mindfulness in everyday life. This begins with recognising the beauty and wisdom embedded in creation. Take a moment each day to observe the world around you—appreciate the intricate details of nature, the kindness in human interactions, and the moments of joy that arise unexpectedly. By intentionally acknowledging these manifestations of Divine qualities, you create a foundation for deeper understanding and connection. This practice of mindfulness not only enriches your experience but also aligns your heart with the essence of Allah's attributes.

Next, engage in self-reflection and personal growth. This involves a sincere examination of your thoughts, actions, and intentions. Set aside time for introspection, asking yourself how closely your behaviours align with the Divine attributes you admire, such as mercy, compassion, and justice. Identify areas for improvement and make a commitment to embody these virtues in your daily interactions. Surround yourself with individuals who inspire you to grow, as the company you keep can significantly influence your journey toward embodying these divine qualities.

Another critical step is to cultivate a spirit of service and generosity. Acts of kindness and charity not only reflect the attribute of generosity but also connect you with others in meaningful ways. Look for opportunities to lend a helping hand to those in need, whether through volunteer work, simple acts of kindness, or sharing your resources. Each act of service is a reflection of Divine mercy and compassion, creating a ripple effect that can inspire others to embody the same attributes. This practice not only enriches the lives of those around you but also deepens your own connection to Allah's essence.

Incorporating prayer and spiritual practices into your daily routine can also facilitate a deeper connection with Allah's attributes. Set aside time for prayer, Quran, contemplation, meditation, or recitation of Divine qualities, allowing these moments to ground you and align your intentions with the Divine. Through these practices, you can cultivate a sense of peace and purpose that nourishes your spirit. Engage in supplication, asking for guidance and strength to embody the virtues you aspire to reflect, creating an ongoing dialogue with Allah (SWT) that fosters growth and understanding.

Finally, share your journey with others and encourage them to explore and embody Divine attributes as well. By discussing your experiences and the transformations you undergo, you inspire those around you to embark on their own paths of discovery. Create spaces for open dialogue, where individuals from different backgrounds can come together to learn about and reflect on these attributes. This collective exploration not only enriches your understanding but also fosters a community that embodies the essence of Allah's beautiful attributes, creating a legacy of compassion, love, and connection that transcends boundaries.

Inspiring Others Through Our Actions

In the intricate tapestry of life, our actions serve as the threads that weave connections between our inner selves and the world around us. Each choice we make, every word we utter, can resonate far beyond our immediate surroundings, creating ripples that inspire and uplift others. This is especially true when we consciously reflect Allah's divine attributes through our conduct. By embodying qualities such as mercy, compassion, and justice, we not only enhance our own spiritual journey but also illuminate the paths of those who witness our actions, inviting them to seek deeper connections with the Divine.

When I think of our beloved shaykh, we recognise that his life was a vivid illustration of these principles in action. Through his unwavering commitment to embodying the virtues of Allah, he became a beacon of hope and inspiration. His humility, patience, and love for all of creation encouraged those around him to reflect on their own behaviours and strive to connect with the Divine through their interactions. He showed us that the most profound teachings of faith are often expressed through simple yet powerful acts of kindness, reminding us that our capacity to inspire others lies in our ability to live out these values authentically and with pride.

Consider the impact of a single act of generosity. When we offer help to someone in need, we not only uplift their spirits but also inspire them to extend that kindness to others. This chain reaction can lead to a community transformed by compassion, echoing the Divine attribute of Al-Raḥmān, the Most Merciful. By being conscious of how our actions reflect Allah's essence, we can cultivate an environment where love and understanding flourish, transcending boundaries of faith and belief. In this way, our actions serve as a living testament to the beauty of creation and the Divine spark that resides within each of us.

Moreover, the challenge lies in maintaining this awareness in our daily lives. It is easy to become absorbed in our own struggles, but when we intentionally shift our focus outward, we discover opportunities to embody the attributes of Allah in even the smallest interactions. A smile, a listening ear, or a moment of patience can serve as powerful reminders of the divine presence in our lives. As we strive to reflect these qualities, we not only grow closer to Allah but also encourage others to embark on their own journeys of self-discovery and spiritual awakening.

Ultimately, inspiring others through our actions is not merely about the impact we make but also about the legacy we leave behind. Our lives can become a source of light for those who seek understanding and connection with the Divine. By embodying the attributes of Allah in our daily interactions, we create a ripple effect that has the potential to touch countless lives, inviting them to witness the beauty of creation and inspiring them to explore their own relationships with faith. In this shared journey, we find common ground, bridging divides and fostering an environment where everyone, regardless of their beliefs, can aspire to illuminate their souls through acts of kindness and love.

Chapter 13:

The Call to Action

Engaging with Creation

Engaging with creation invites us to embark on a profound journey of connection, not just with the world around us, but with Allah's essence as reflected through His Divine attributes. Every tree, every river, and every creature serves as a testament to His infinite wisdom, mercy, and beauty. In this delicate dance of existence, we find a mirror that reflects the qualities of our Creator, urging us to open our hearts and minds to the lessons hidden in plain sight. This invitation to see is a call for all, regardless of faith or belief, to appreciate the divine fabric woven into the tapestry of life.

Our beloved shaykh has illuminated this path for many, demonstrating how to perceive the Divine attributes manifesting in the world. His teachings encourage us to witness the mercy of Allah in the gentle rustle of leaves, the compassion in the eyes of a stray animal, and the wisdom in the cycles of nature. By cultivating a deeper awareness of these attributes, we learn to recognise our own potential for embodying such virtues in our daily lives. This relationship with creation becomes a living testament to our innate yearning for connection with the Divine, guiding us toward a more compassionate and understanding existence.

As we engage with creation, we also discover the interconnectedness of all beings, a principle that transcends religious boundaries. This universal thread reminds us that every soul, regardless of its background, is part of the same Divine design. By fostering a sense of unity with our surroundings, we can celebrate diversity while recognising the shared essence that binds us. This perspective encourages not only respect for all forms of life but also a commitment to stewardship, nurturing the world as a reflection of Allah's love and care.

In embodying the virtues we observe in creation, we become active participants in the unfolding story of life. Each act of kindness, each moment of understanding, and each instance of gratitude strengthens our connection to the divine attributes we wish to reflect. This journey is not limited to the devout; it is an open invitation for everyone to explore the beauty and wisdom found in everyday experiences. As we reflect on these moments, we realise that our actions can illuminate the path for others, inspiring them to engage in their own journey of discovery.

Ultimately, engaging with creation is an invitation to deepen our relationship with Allah, to see Him in every corner of existence, and to embody His attributes in our interactions with others. It is a call to reflect on our role within this magnificent ecosystem and to embrace the responsibility that comes with it. As we learn to see the Divine in creation, we also learn to see the Divine within ourselves and each other, fostering a world where compassion, mercy, and love reign supreme. In this shared journey, we can all find common ground, transcending differences and uniting in our quest to understand and manifest the essence of Allah in our lives.

Inviting Others to Reflect on Divine Beauty

Inviting others to reflect on Divine beauty is a journey that transcends boundaries, inviting every individual—Muslim, non-Muslim, or those who identify with no faith—to engage with the essence of creation and the attributes of Allah (SWT). Each of us is surrounded by manifestations of beauty that echo the Divine, encouraging moments of introspection and connection. In this exploration, we are called to witness the intricate details of the world around us, from a delicate flower to a vast starry sky, realising that these elements serve as mirrors reflecting Allah's attributes such as mercy, wisdom, and beauty.

The teachings of my beloved shaykh illuminate this path, guiding us to recognise that the beauty of creation is not merely aesthetic but a profound reminder of the Creator's presence. Through his wisdom, we learn to observe the world with a heart open to reflection, prompting us to see beyond the surface of existence. He has shown us that each moment of beauty is an invitation to deepen our understanding of Allah's essence, urging us to embody the virtues we discern. In recognising the divine attributes manifested in our surroundings, we are inspired to cultivate these qualities within ourselves.

In the rush of daily life, it is easy to overlook the signs of Divine beauty that surround us. Yet, my shaykh encourages a mindful approach, prompting us to pause and reflect. By intentionally seeking out beauty in the mundane, we can transform our perspective, allowing the Divine to seep into our consciousness. This practice of reflection not only enriches our spiritual lives but also fosters gratitude, humility, and a sense of wonder. By inviting others to join in this reflection, we create a shared space for dialogue, where diverse perspectives can enrich our understanding of the divine.

Furthermore, the act of inviting others to reflect on Divine beauty serves as a powerful unifying force. Regardless of one's beliefs, the appreciation of beauty is a universal experience. It fosters connections between people, inviting conversations that transcend theological differences and cultivate mutual respect. In this shared journey, we discover that the quest for understanding Allah's attributes is a common thread that binds humanity together. Each person's insights and experiences contribute to a richer tapestry of collective spirituality that honours the diversity of creation.

Ultimately, reflecting on divine beauty offers a pathway to personal transformation and collective harmony. As we embrace this invitation, we become agents of change, embodying the virtues we discern in the world around us. By nurturing a spirit of reflection and appreciation, we not only deepen our relationship with Allah (SWT) but also inspire others to embark on their own journeys of discovery. This is an invitation to see, to feel, and to embody the Divine attributes that connect us all, creating a world that resonates with the beauty of Allah's essence.

Chapter 14:

A Legacy of Light

Continuing the Journey Beyond the Book

Continuing the journey beyond the pages of "Illuminated Souls: Finding Allah's Essence in Creation" invites each reader to immerse themselves in a transformative experience that transcends the written word. The teachings of my beloved shaykh serve as a beacon of light, illuminating the path toward recognising Allah's Divine attributes reflected in every aspect of creation. This journey is not limited to a specific faith; it is an invitation for all—Muslims, non-Muslims, and those without any religious beliefs—to discover the beauty of existence and the virtues that lie within. By embracing these Divine qualities, we can cultivate a deeper connection with ourselves and the world around us.

As we continue this journey, let us reflect on the profound influence of my shaykh's teachings. His wisdom encourages us to see beyond the surface of things, urging us to perceive the Divine essence that permeates all creation. By understanding the attributes of Allah—such as mercy, compassion, and justice—we can find inspiration in the simplest of moments. A gentle breeze, a child's laughter, or the colours of a sunset can serve as reminders of these attributes, urging us to embody them in our daily lives. This awareness not only enhances our spiritual growth but also fosters a sense of connection with others, bridging divides and nurturing empathy.

The journey beyond the book requires active participation in our lives. It is about embodying the virtues we have come to recognise and striving to reflect them in our actions. Each interaction with others becomes an opportunity to practice kindness, patience, and understanding. Whether in our families, workplaces, or communities, let us be the vessels of Allah's attributes, allowing His essence to shine through us. This commitment to living these values not only enriches our own lives but creates ripples of positive change in the world around us.

Moreover, this journey is not a solitary endeavour. Engaging with a community that shares similar aspirations can amplify our growth. Whether through study circles, charitable initiatives, or interfaith dialogues, being part of a collective effort fosters deeper understanding and connection. Sharing experiences and insights allows us to learn from one another, reminding us that we are all part of a greater tapestry of creation. In this interconnectedness, we find strength and support, encouraging each other to remain steadfast on the path toward embodying Divine attributes.

Ultimately, the journey beyond the book is a lifelong commitment to seeking Allah's essence in all that we encounter. It invites us to remain curious, to ask questions, and to continuously explore the depth of our existence. As we reflect on the teachings of my shaykh and integrate them into our lives, we are reminded that this journey is not just about reaching a destination but about the experiences we gather along the way. The people we meet and inspire. Each step taken in faith, no matter how small, brings us closer to understanding the profound beauty of creation and the Divine attributes of Allah, enriching our lives and the lives of those around us.

Sharing the Message with Future Generations

As we reflect on the beauty of Allah's creation and His Divine attributes, it becomes imperative that we pass on this understanding to future generations. The essence of our faith, as illuminated by the teachings of my shaykh, resonates deeply with the hearts of those who seek connection with the Divine. By sharing this message, we not only honour our own spiritual journeys but also empower the next generation to discover their own paths to Allah. This transmission of wisdom transcends religious boundaries, inviting everyone—Muslims, non-Muslims, and those exploring their beliefs—to appreciate the profound connection between creation and the Creator.

In an ever-evolving world, where distractions abound and spiritual disconnection can easily take root, the role of mentorship becomes vital. My shaykh exemplified the importance of nurturing young hearts and minds, guiding them to recognise the signs of Allah in the world around them. By fostering a sense of curiosity and reverence for creation, we can inspire future generations to see beyond the material and to explore the spiritual dimensions of existence. This is not merely a religious duty; it is a universal call to recognise the shared human experience of seeking purpose and meaning.

As we share this message, we must also embody the virtues that we wish to impart. The attributes of Allah—such as compassion, mercy, and wisdom—should be reflected in our interactions with others. Future generations will learn not only through our words but also through our actions. When they witness kindness, patience, and understanding, they are more likely to internalise these qualities and carry them forward. This embodiment of Divine attributes serves as a living testament to the teachings of my shaykh, creating a ripple effect that extends far beyond our immediate communities and long after we are gone.

Education plays a crucial role in this transmission of knowledge. We must strive to create environments—both formal and informal—where discussions about the Divine can flourish. This can be achieved through community gatherings, educational programs, and interfaith dialogues that celebrate our shared values. By engaging individuals from diverse backgrounds in meaningful conversations about Allah's attributes, we cultivate a culture of respect and understanding. This is how we ensure that the message of love and connection with the Divine remains alive and relevant in the hearts of future generations.

Ultimately, sharing the message of Allah's essence in creation is a collective endeavour that requires our active participation. It is a journey of love, curiosity, and commitment to the truth that transcends all differences. By guiding future generations to see the beauty of Allah reflected in the world, we not only enrich their lives but also contribute to a more harmonious and compassionate society. Let us take up this sacred responsibility, inspired by the teachings of my shaykh, as we illuminate the hearts and minds of those who will carry the torch of faith into the future.

Chapter 15:

Conclusion: The Eternal Connection

The Lifelong Journey of Seeking Allah's Essence

The pursuit of Allah's essence is a journey that transcends the boundaries of faith, culture, and personal belief systems. For Muslims, it is a sacred obligation; for non-Muslims, it can become a path of introspection and discovery. This lifelong quest invites individuals to explore the depths of their own existence while seeking the Divine attributes that permeate all of creation. Every interaction with the world around us becomes an opportunity to recognise Allah's endless qualities, from His Compassion evident in the kindness of strangers to His Majesty mirrored in the vastness of the cosmos. Each moment serves as a reminder that we are part of a greater tapestry, woven together by the threads of Divine love and mercy.

The influence of a spiritual guide, or shaykh, can illuminate this journey, acting as a beacon for those navigating the complexities of their spiritual path. Through their teachings, we are encouraged to look beyond the surface of everyday life and to engage with the deeper meanings that lie within. My beloved shaykh has shown me that every tree, every star, and every heartbeat is a reflection of Allah's attributes. Their wisdom inspires us to cultivate these virtues within ourselves, fostering a sense of connection that is both profound and transformative. By embodying qualities such as patience, generosity, and forgiveness, we not only enhance our relationship with Allah but also with those around us.

As we embark on this lifelong journey, we are reminded that the search for Allah's essence is not confined to formal rituals or sacred texts. Instead, it unfolds in the simplicity of our everyday experiences. A walk in nature, a moment of silence, or a heartfelt conversation can all serve as gateways to deeper understanding. When we approach these moments with mindfulness and intention, we begin to see the Divine fingerprints in everything around us. This perspective transforms our interactions, encouraging us to engage with the world from a place of gratitude and reverence, recognising that the essence of Allah is present in all that exists.

Moreover, this journey is not one of isolation but rather a communal experience that invites dialogue and shared understanding. Engaging with people from various backgrounds enriches our perspectives and helps us appreciate the diverse ways in which Allah's attributes manifest in different cultures and traditions. Each person carries unique insights that can enhance our own understanding of the Divine. By fostering an environment of mutual respect, we create a space where the essence of Allah can be discussed and celebrated, allowing us all to grow together on this shared path of discovery.

Ultimately, the lifelong journey of seeking Allah's essence is an invitation to awaken our souls to the beauty that surrounds us. It encourages each of us, regardless of our personal beliefs, to reflect on the Divine qualities we wish to embody in our lives. As we strive to align ourselves with these attributes, we not only transform our own hearts but also contribute positively to the world around us. This journey is not merely about seeking enlightenment; it is about becoming a source of light for others, guiding them to see the reflections of Allah within themselves and in creation. Thus, we become part of a larger movement that seeks to illuminate the world through the beauty of Divine attributes.

The Transformative Power of Divine Attributes

The exploration of divine attributes serves as a powerful invitation to perceive the beauty of Allah's essence reflected in all aspects of creation. Each attribute, from the Compassionate to the Just, calls us closer to understanding the profound nature of the Divine. As we embark on this journey, we recognise that every element of the universe, from the smallest grain of sand to the vastness of the cosmos, mirrors these Divine qualities. By cultivating an awareness of these attributes, we can begin to see the interconnectedness of all life, fostering a deeper respect for our surroundings and a greater appreciation for the Creator's artistry.

My beloved shaykh exemplifies the transformative power of embodying Allah's attributes. Through his teachings, we learn that compassion is not merely an emotion but a way to transcend religious boundaries. He encourages us to practice empathy and kindness, reminding us that these virtues resonate deeply within human nature. As I witnessed his actions—his unwavering patience, his gentle words, and his selfless service—we are inspired to reflect on how we can embody these Divine qualities in our daily lives. The shaykh becomes a living testament to the idea that when we align ourselves with these attributes, we contribute to a more harmonious and loving world.

The Divine Attributes of Allah

99 Names of Allah

ALLAH	Allah
AR-RAHMAN	The Most Compassionate, The Beneficent, The Gracious
AR-RAHIM	The Merciful
AL-MALIK	The King
AL-QUDDOS	The Most Holy
AS-SALAAM	The All-Peaceful, The Bestower of Peace
AL-MU-MIN	The Granter of Security
AL-MUHAYMIN	The Protector
AL-AZIZ	The Mighty
AL-JABBAR	The Compeller
AL-MUTAKABBIR	Supreme In Greatness, The Majestic
AL-KHALIQ	The Creator
AL-BARI	The Maker
AL-MUSAWWIR	The Bestower of Form, The Shaper
AL-GAFFAR	The Forgiver
AL-QAHHAR	The Subduer
AL-WAHHAB	The Bestower
AR-RAZZAQ	The Provider
AL-FATTAH	The Opener, The Judge
AL-ALIM	The All-Knowing
AL-QABID	The Withholder
AL-BASIT	The Expander
AL-KHAFID	The Abaser
AR-RAFI	The Exalter
AL-MU'IZZ	The Bestower of Honour
AL-MUDHILL	The Humiliator
AS-SAMI	The All-Hearing
AL-BASIR	The All-Seeing
AL-HAKAM	The Judge
AL-ADL	The Just, The Equitable
AL-LATIF	The Gentle, The Knower of Subtleties
AL-KHABIR	The All-Aware
AL-HALIM	The Forbearing
AL-AZIM	The Incomparably Great
AL-GAFUR	The Forgiving
ASH-SHAKUR	The Appreciative
AL-ALIYY	The Most High
AL-KABIR	The Most Great
AL-HAFIZ	The Preserver
AL-MUGHITH	The Sustainer
AL-HASIB	The Reckoner
AL-JALIL	The Majestic, The Revered, The Sublime
AL-KARIM	The Generous
AR-RAQIB	The Watchful
AL-MUJIB	The Responsive
AL-WASI	The All-Encompassing, The All-Embracing
AL-HAKIM	The Wise
AL-WADUD	The Loving One
AL-MAJEED	(The Most Glorious)
AL-BA'ITH	The Resurrector
ASH-SHAHID	The Witness
AL-HAQQ	The Truth
AL-WAKIL	The Ultimate Trustee, The Disposer of Affairs
AL-QAWIYY	The Most Strong
AL-MATIN	The Firm One, The Authoritative
AL-WALIYY	The Protector
AL-HAMID	The All-Praised, The Praiseworthy
AL-MUHSI	The Reckoner
AL-MUBDI	The Originator
AL-MU'ID	The Restorer of Life
AL-MUHYI	The Giver of Life
AL-MUMIT	The Causer of Death
AL-HAYY	The Ever-Living
AL-QAYYUM	The Self-Existing by Whom All Subsist
AL-WAJID	The Self-Sufficient, The All-Perceiving
AL-MAJID	(The Glorified)
AL-WAHID	The One
AS-SAMAD	The Eternally Besought
AL-QADIR	The Omnipotent, The Able
AL-MUQTADIR	The Powerful
AL-MUQADDIM	The Expediter
AL-MU'AKHKHIR	The Delayer
AL-AWWAL	The First
AL-AKHIR	The Last
AL-ZAAHIR	The Manifest
AL-BATIN	The Hidden
AL-WALI	The Governer, The Protector
AL-MUTA'ALI	The Most Exalted
AL-BARR	The Doer of Good
AT-TAWWAB	The Granter & Accepter of Repentance
AL-MUNTAQIM	The Lord of Retribution, The Avenger
AL-AFUWW	The Pardoner
AR-RA'UF	The Most Kind, The Clement
MALIK-UL-MULK	Owner of Kingdom
DHUL JALAL WAL IKRAM	Possessor of Majesty & Honour
AL-MUQSIT	The Equitable
AL-JA'ME	The Gatherer
AL-GHANIYY	The All-Sufficient
AL-MUGHNI	The Enricher
AL-MAANI	The Preventer of Harm
AD-DARR	The Afflicter
AN-NAFI	The Benefiter
AN-NUR	The Light
AL-HADI	The Guide
AL-BA'DI	The Originator
AL-BAQI	The Everlasting
AL-WARITH	The Ultimate Inheritor
AR-RASHID	The Guide
AS-SABUR	The Patient One

www.ingramcontent.com/pod-product-compliance
Lightning Source LLC
Chambersburg PA
CBHW041117070526
44584CB00002B/195